Take Me Out to the Ball Game

Dennis Fertig

Photographs by Wm. Franklin McMahon

Albert Whitman & Company
Niles, Illinois

To Michael, who loves the game, and Margaret, who likes it . . . sort of *D.F.*

To Jonathan, looking forward to his first baseball game *W.F.M.*

Text © 1987 by Dennis Fertig
Photographs © 1987 by Albert Whitman & Company
Design by Gordon Stromberg
Published in 1987 by Albert Whitman & Company, Niles, Illinois
Published simultaneously in Canada by
General Publishing, Limited, Toronto
All rights reserved. Printed in U.S.A.
10 9 8 7 6 5 4 3 2 1

Library of Congress Cataloging-in-Publication Data
Fertig, Dennis.
    Take me out to the ball game.

    Summary: Describes in text and photographs a young boy's experiences as he attends his first major league baseball game at Chicago's Wrigley Field with his father.
    1. Baseball—Illinois—Chicago—Juvenile literature.
[1. Baseball—Illinois—Chicago] I. McMahon, William Franklin, ill. II. Title.
GV867.5.F47 1987   796.357'64'0977311   86-26642
ISBN 0-8075-7735-9

My name's Ryan. I like to play and watch baseball, especially with my dad.

My favorite team is the Chicago Cubs. My dad says his favorite is my Little League team. The Cubs are his second favorite.

One day, my dad had a big surprise for me. He had two tickets to see the Chicago Cubs play the Atlanta Braves. One ticket was for him and one for me.

On the day of the game, we took the train to the ball park. The ride was fun. Right before we got off, my dad showed me Wrigley Field. That's where the Chicago Cubs play ball.

A few minutes after we left the train station, we were in front of Wrigley Field.

A lot was going on outside the park.

When we got inside, the first thing we did was buy a scorecard. A scorecard tells you the name and number of each player. Even my dad doesn't know all the players' numbers by heart.

Wow! I was surprised when I saw the field. My dad said the sky is bluer and the grass greener at Wrigley Field than anywhere else in Chicago.

The walls in the outfield are covered with ivy.

Behind the park are houses. People on the roofs of the houses can see into the park.

The game hadn't started yet, so my dad took me down closer to the field to watch the players practice.

This was a really special day for me. I got to meet Bobby Dernier, the Cubs' centerfielder. He signed his name on my glove. From now on, Bobby Dernier is my favorite player!

On the way to our seats, my dad bought me a pennant.

Soon practice was over for both the Cubs and the Braves. The grounds crew got the field ready for the game.

Then everybody sang "The Star-Spangled Banner," even the umpires and the players in the dugout. I didn't know all the words. But that was okay, because I liked listening to my dad sing.

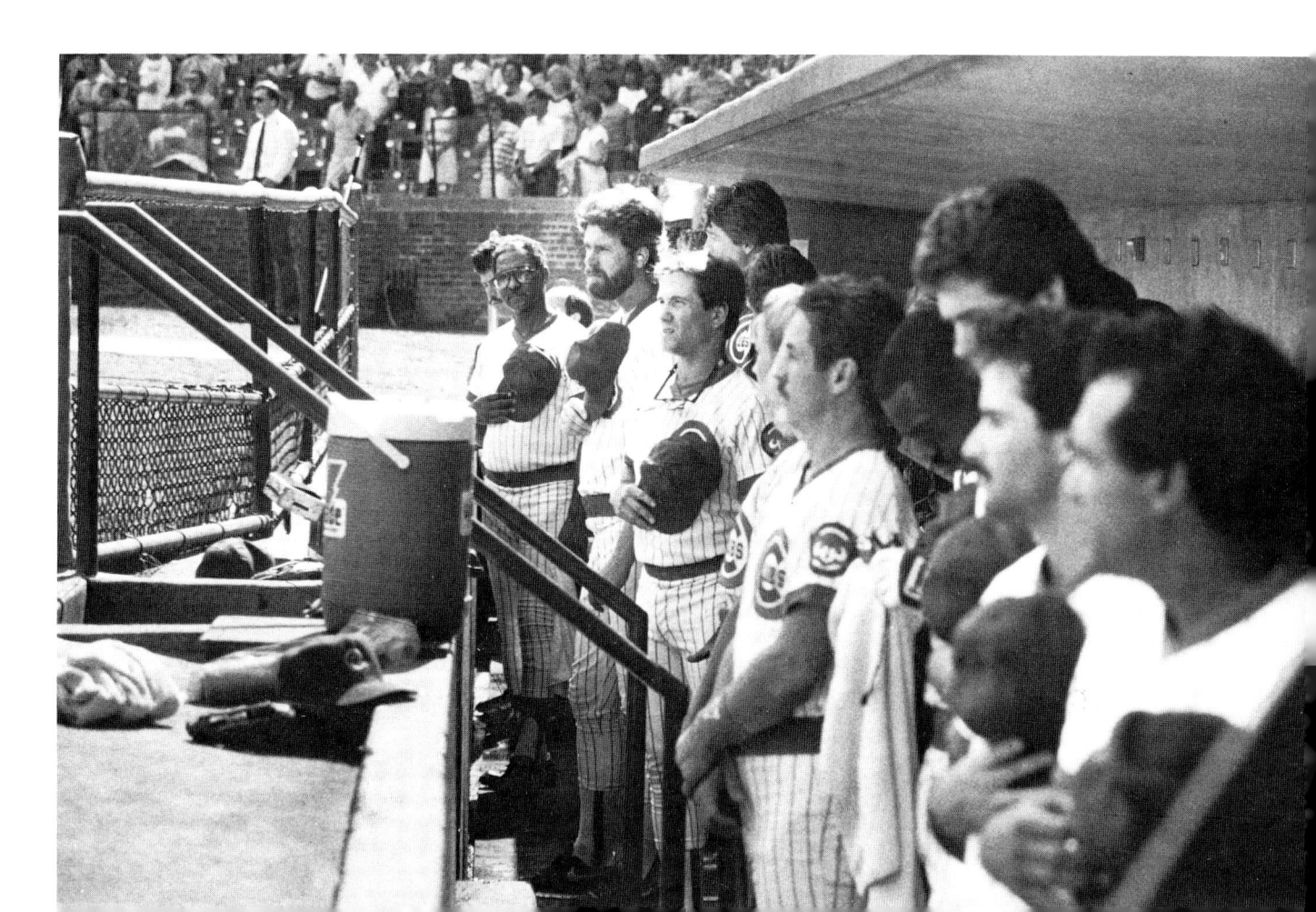

After the singing, the umpire yelled, "Play ball!"

The game started with the Braves at bat. The Cubs' pitcher could really throw the ball! He struck out the first three Atlanta batters.

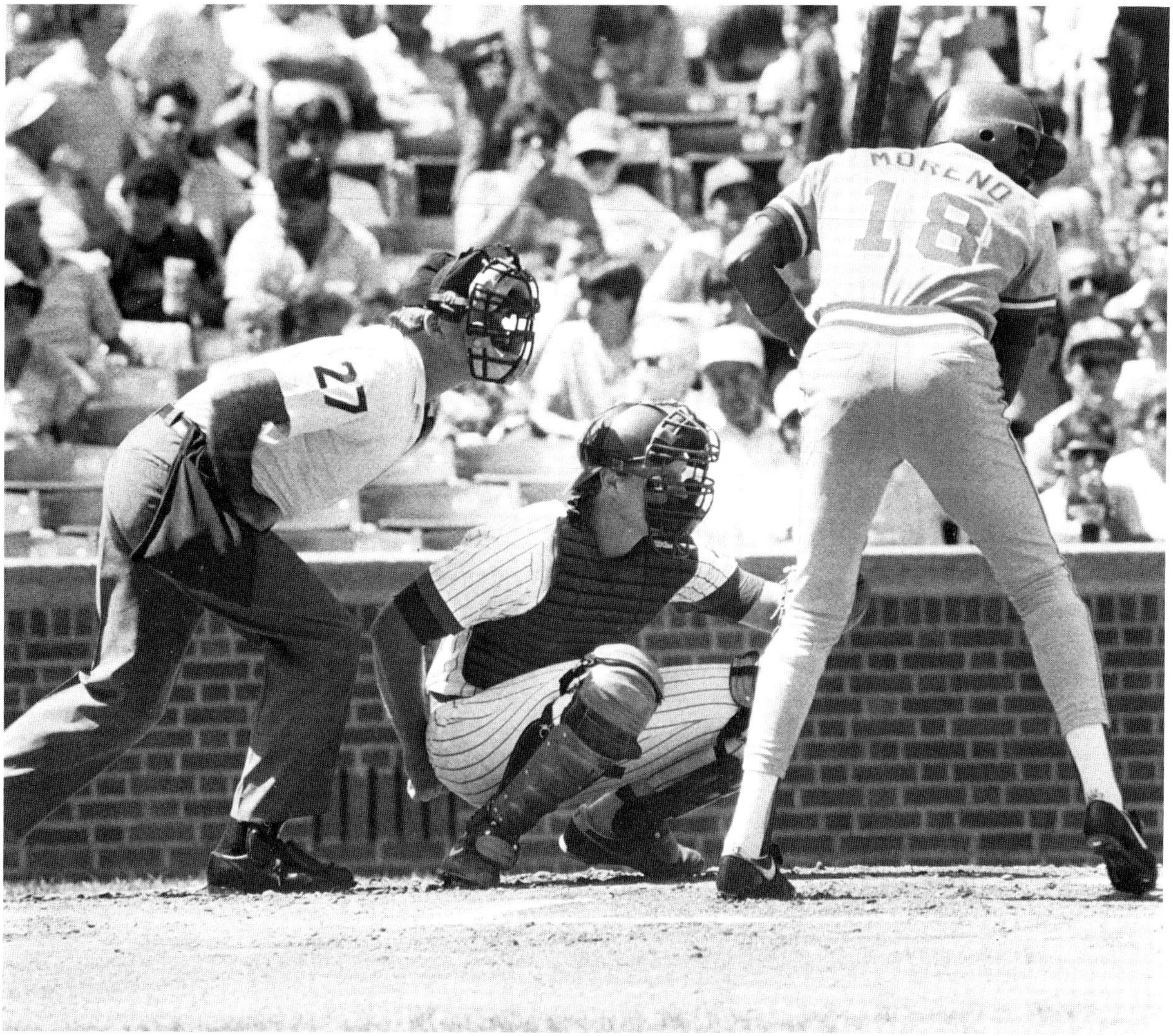
MORENO
18
27

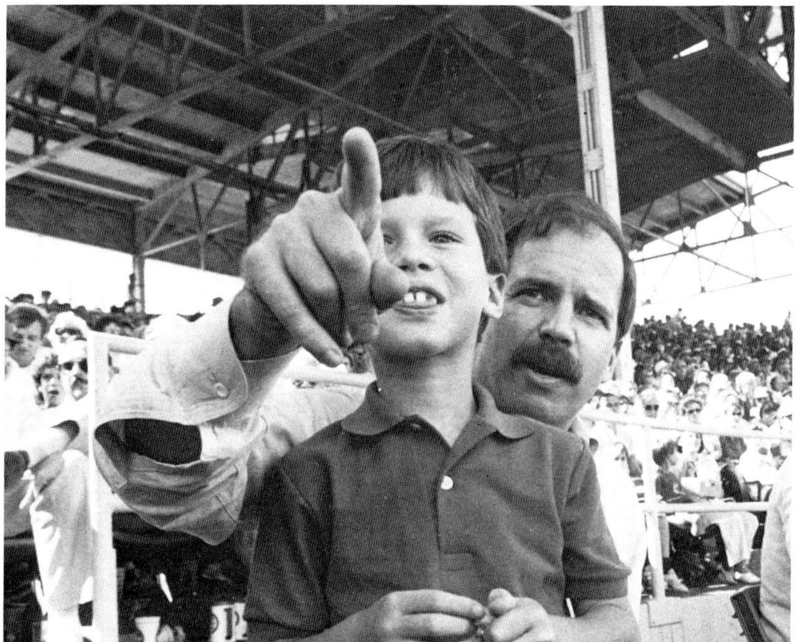

When it was the Cubs' turn to bat, they scored a run. Cubs 1, Braves 0.

I told my dad the Cubs were going to win. He said he hoped so, but it was too early to tell for sure.

Pretty soon, the Braves scored a run, too. The game was tied. Cubs 1, Braves 1.

During the game, lots of people were selling all kinds of food. I was getting hungry, so my dad bought me some peanuts.

It was hard for me to break open the peanut shells. But my dad could.

When the Cubs were at bat again, my dad told me a secret about the Wrigley Field scoreboard. There are people inside it who change the numbers every time a team scores a run.

While we were looking, Bobby Dernier's name flashed on the screen. That meant he was up to bat.

Bobby swung the bat and smacked the ball. It flew over the shortstop's head. It was a hit!

The next Cubs' batter smacked the ball hard, too. I thought for sure he had hit a home run. The ball was going, going, going . . . But a Braves' outfielder caught it.

Bobby Dernier didn't get a chance to score. When the inning ended, the score was still Cubs 1, Braves 1.

The next time the Braves were at bat, a funny thing happened. One of the Braves hit a ball that got stuck in the ivy. My dad said that meant the batter could only go to second base.

I guess the next Braves' batter, Dale Murphy, didn't want the ball he hit to get stuck, too. He socked it over the ivy and out of the park.

A home run! The runner on second base scored first. The Braves were winning 3 to 1.

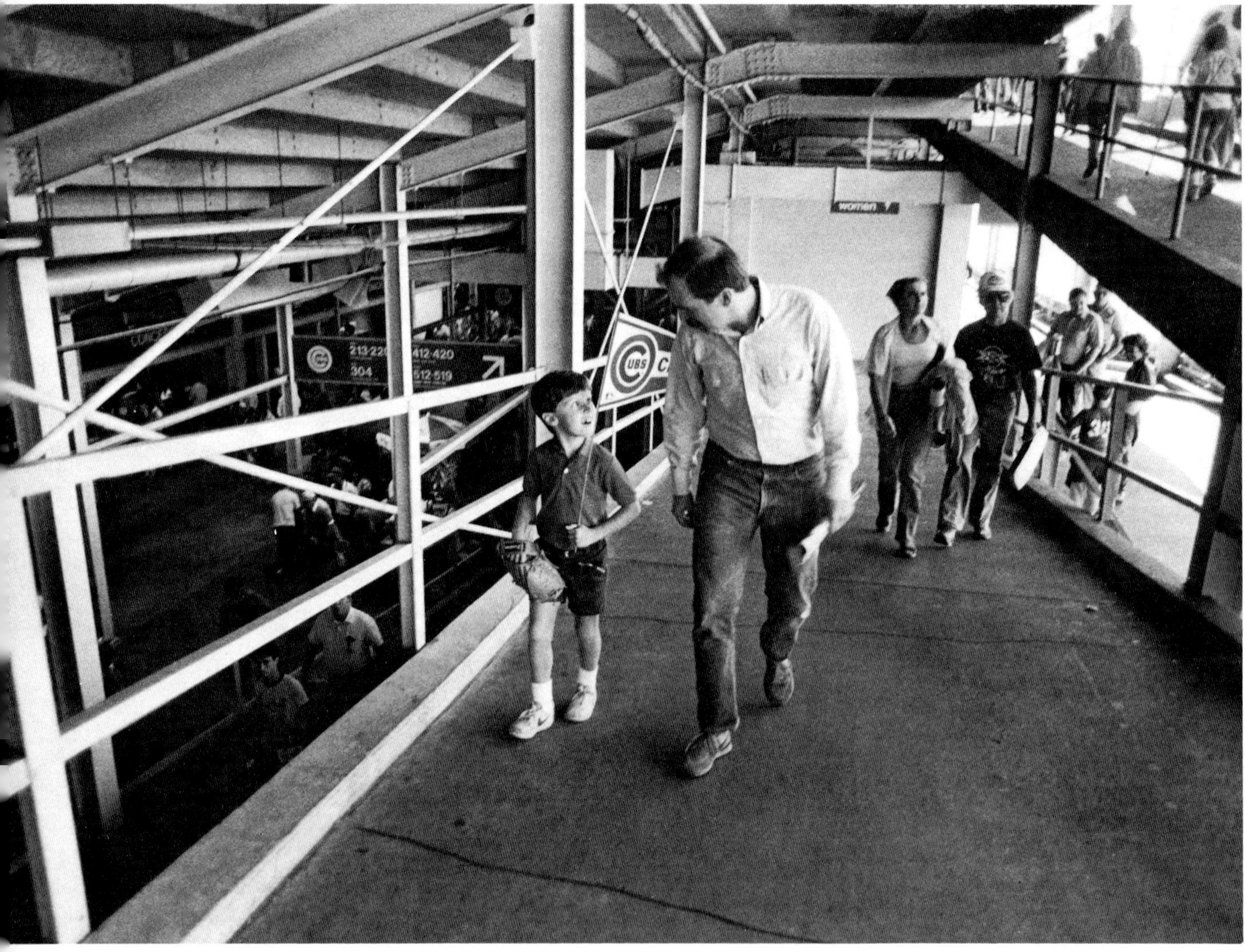

women
213-220
412-420
304
512-519
CUBS

My Dad could tell that I was getting tired of sitting. "Time to go exploring!" he said.

As we walked up a ramp underneath the stands, I pretended we were climbing a mountain. Near the top, we saw the TV announcer's booth and a TV camera. I hoped my mom and baby sister could see us on television.

When we came back to our seats, the Braves scored another run. Now they were winning by even more. Braves 4, Cubs 1.

I didn't like it too much when the Cubs were losing. For a while, I played with some of the toy monsters I'd brought in my backpack.

After that my dad showed me how to enjoy a game even if your favorite team is losing. You should look for interesting plays.

We watched the Cubs' pitcher try to stop a Braves' runner from stealing a base.

Then something really exciting happened. I almost caught a foul ball. My dad said he's gone to a lot of ball games, but he has never, *ever* caught a foul ball. I think he would really like to.

After a while, it looked like the Braves were going to score even more runs. But the Cubs made some great plays. They even tagged Dale Murphy out when he tried to steal second base.

I asked my dad if he remembered the time I almost tagged someone out at second in a Little League game. He did.

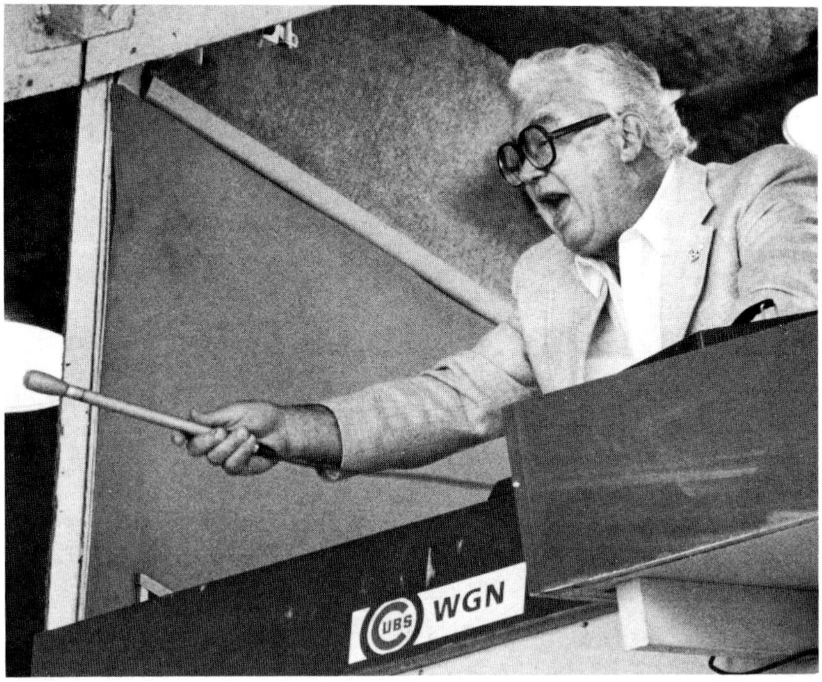

CUBS WGN

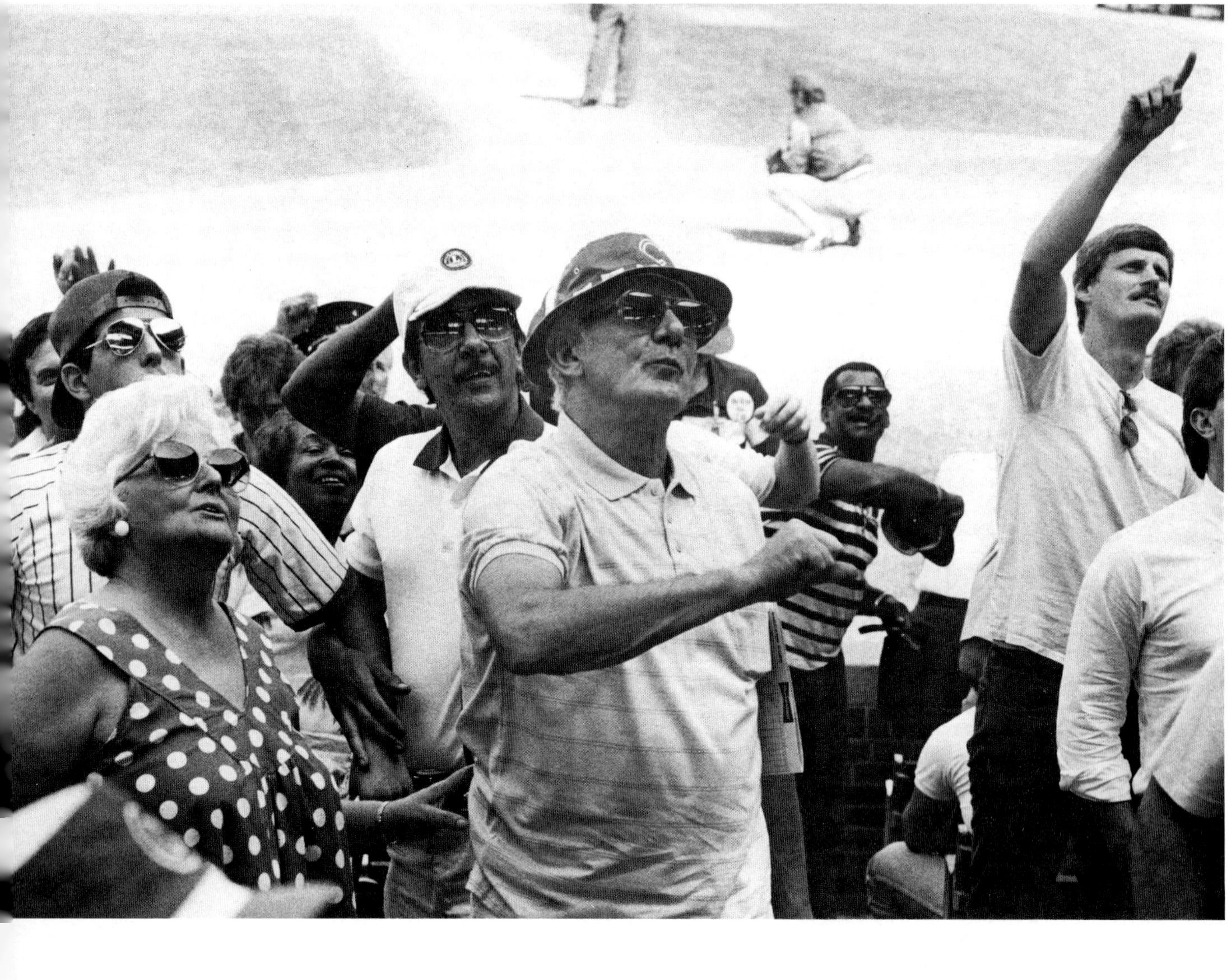

In the seventh inning, the TV announcer leaned out of the booth and yelled to all the Cub fans to sing. We sang "Take Me Out to the Ball Game." This time I think my dad was listening to *me* sing.

Pretty soon it was the Cubs' very last chance to bat. When the first two Cubs made outs, everyone thought the Atlanta Braves would win.

But the crowd cheered when the Cubs got a hit. The crowd cheered even louder when the Cubs got another hit and scored a run. Braves 4, Cubs 2.

When *another* Cub batter got a hit, the crowd really went wild. The organ played music that sounded like a drum—

BOOM,

   Boom,

  Boom,

 Boom.

It got higher—

BOOM,

   Boom,

  Boom,

 Boom.

And higher—

BOOM,

   # Boom,

  # Boom,

 # Boom.

One of the Cubs' best batters was up. He smashed a ball into the outfield. A Cub scored. Another Cub raced toward home plate. Just as he slid into home, the catcher tagged him. He was out! The Cubs lost 4 to 3.

Later, a flag was raised above the scoreboard. It had a letter "L" on it to show that the Cubs had lost.

I was a little sad, but I still had lots of fun. My dad said that no matter who won, he liked seeing his second favorite team play, especially when he was with his favorite player. He meant me.

I can't wait to go to Wrigley Field again. Next time, I'll catch a foul ball, and I'll give it to my dad.